ESTHER
Didn't Dream of Being
QUEEN

by Allison Ofanansky

illustrated by Valentina Belloni

APPLES & HONEY PRESS

To the women in the Tzfat megillah
reading-and-writing group.
And to everyone who stands up
to a challenge even when afraid.
—AO

To my daughter Vittoria, may you always
be as brave and strong as Esther.
—VB

Apples & Honey Press
An Imprint of Behrman House
Millburn, New Jersey 07041
www.applesandhoneypress.com

Text copyright © 2021 by Allison Ofanansky
Illustrations copyright © 2021 by Behrman House
ISBN 978-1-68115-561-6

Library of Congress Cataloging-in-Publication Data
Names: Ofanansky, Allison, author. | Belloni, Valentina, illustrator.
Title: Esther didn't dream of being queen / Allison Ofanansky ; illustrated by Valentina Belloni.
Description: Millburn : Apples & Honey Press, 2021. | Summary: "In this
lively retelling of the Purim story, Queen Esther finds the courage to
save the Jewish people from Haman, the king's evil advisor"—Provided by publisher.
Identifiers: LCCN 2020003669 | ISBN 9781681155616 (hardcover)
Subjects: LCSH: Purim"—Juvenile literature. | Bible. Esther"—Juvenile literature.
Classification: LCC BM695.P8 O33 2021 | DDC 222/.909505"—dc23
LC record available at https://lccn.loc.gov/2020003669

The illustrations in this book were created using digital techniques. The artist sketched directly on the computer
with a pen tablet, then finalized the art by adding digital brushstrokes, patterns, and textures.

Designed by Michelle Martinez
Edited by Alef Davis and Dena Neusner
Printed in China
1 3 5 7 9 8 6 4 2

022134.1K1/B1634/A7

Once upon a time, in a kingdom far, far away,
I was an orphan girl who became queen.

No, I'm not Cinderella. My name is Esther,
and my story is not a fairy tale.

I'll start again.

Once upon a time, in a kingdom that stretched from India to Ethiopia, I was an orphan girl who never dreamed of being queen. Cousin Mordecai raised me in a small house near the palace. I spent my days digging in my garden, giggling with friends, daydreaming under the olive tree.

I had a nice, quiet life . . .

. . . until the day a royal guard pounded on our door.

"Oh, no! He's probably delivering invitations to one of the king's rowdy parties." I hid in the back room.

"All pretty young women must come to the palace," the messenger told Cousin Mordecai. "The king needs to choose a new queen."

I stifled a gasp. The rumors were true! The king had gotten rid of his queen because she disobeyed his orders. He didn't sound like my idea of Prince Charming.

I decided I wasn't entering his royal beauty contest.

For three years, I avoided the patrols rounding up young women throughout the kingdom. But one spring morning, I just had to get out for a walk. I put on my ugliest dress and messed up my hair.

"Hey there!" A guard had spotted me. "I bet the king would like to meet a nice girl like you." He hustled me into the royal carriage.

"The king won't want a poor orphan as queen," I protested.

"He'll decide whom he wants. I'm just following orders," he said.
A few tears slipped down my cheeks as the
carriage pulled away from the
market.

Cousin Mordecai dashed over and whispered, "Don't
tell anyone who you are or where you're from."

I trusted Cousin Mordecai, so I took his advice and didn't tell anyone at the palace I was Jewish. But it felt strange to hide who I was.

The guard took me to special chambers, crowded with beautiful women from across the kingdom. We were supposed to spend our time getting primped, prettied, and perfumed.

I lit my Shabbat candles in secret and whispered
Hebrew prayers, hoping the king would pick
someone else to be queen.

Each day, one of us was taken to meet the king. While getting ready, she could ask the servants for anything to make herself more beautiful.

"This scarf brings out the color of my eyes. The king is sure to choose me."

"A diamond tiara is pretty, but I want to wear the crown!"

"Don't I look lovely in this dress? No doubt I'll be the next queen."

My turn came. A servant offered me a silk gown.

"I'd rather wear my own clothes," I said.

"An emerald necklace? A fur cape?" he asked.

"No, thank you."

"How would you like your hair done?"

"It's fine like this."

A guard took me to the throne room. The king stared at my plain clothing. I kept my eyes down and refused to smile. I wasn't trying to impress him. I guess that impressed him.

"My new queen!"

Cinderella's fairy tale ends when she marries Prince Charming and they live happily ever after. But when I became queen, my story was only beginning.

I moved into the fancy royal suite, but I missed my simple home.

I even missed the chatter and laughter of the women's chambers.
But when I found out the women still waiting there were going
to be kept as servants, I gave my first royal order:

"Let them go."

I had to stay in the palace,
but I could help others
return home.

I was lonely in the big, cold palace. I tried making friends with the cook, but she just curtsied and called me "Your Highness."

The gardener wouldn't let me get my hands dirty.

At least Cousin Mordecai came by
every day to ask how I was doing.

I hardly ever saw the king. He spent all his time with his favorite advisor, Haman, who was a real bully.

Haman insisted that everyone bow to him, but Cousin Mordecai refused. I watched proudly from the balcony when he told Haman, **"Jews don't bow to people."**

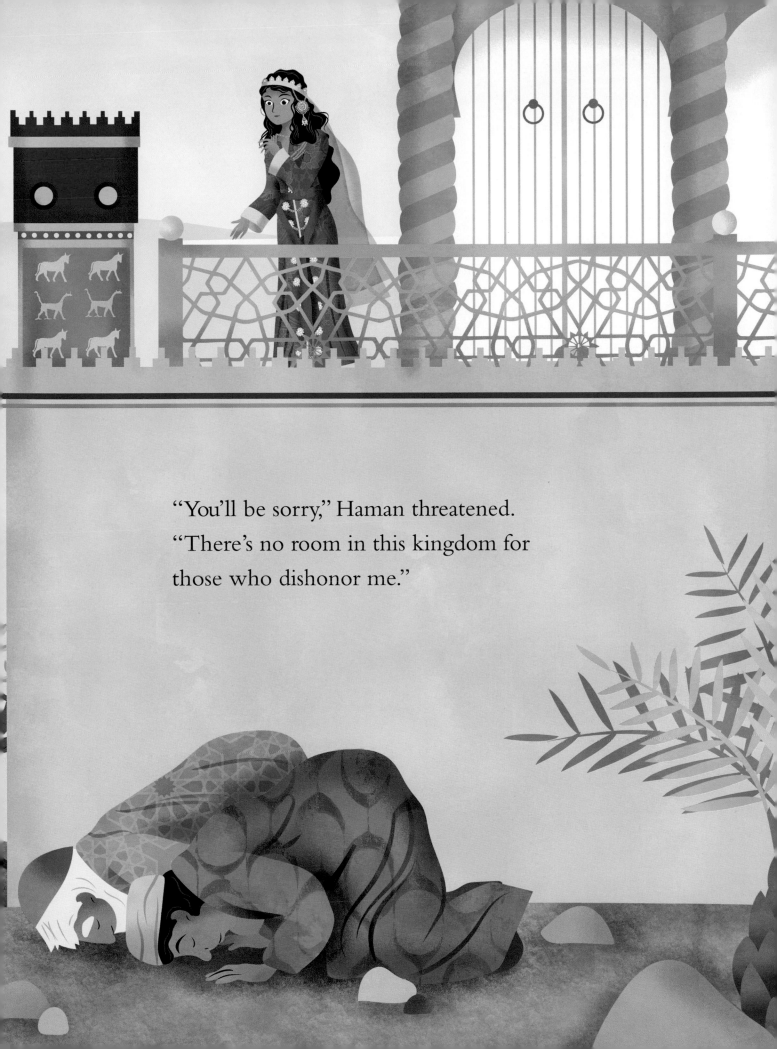

"You'll be sorry," Haman threatened.
"There's no room in this kingdom for
those who dishonor me."

A few days later, Cousin Mordecai came to the palace gates. I'd never seen him so upset.

"What's wrong?" I asked.

"Haman has planned an attack against the Jews throughout the kingdom. We'll all be wiped out—men, women, children." He showed me a letter stamped with the king's seal.

I trembled as I read the order. "Why would the king agree to something so horrible?"

"Haman bribed him. You must convince the king to stop this attack."

"Why me? The king got rid of his first queen. What if he gets angry at me, too?"

"You can save us, Esther. I believe in you!"

I wished I could go home and hide. But I knew I had to try.

I didn't have a fairy godmother to wave a magic wand and solve my problems.

For three days, I tried to work up the courage to approach the king. Finally, I tiptoed down the hallway, terrified. I thought about all the people counting on me. "You're a queen now," I told myself. "Act like one."

I stood up straight, took a deep breath, and walked to the throne room.

"Esther! Come in!" the king said. I almost fainted with relief. "Ask for anything—up to half my kingdom."

I didn't want half his kingdom, but I couldn't blurt out that his favorite advisor was a scoundrel. I had to act carefully.

"Will you and Haman join me for dinner tonight?" I asked.

"With pleasure."

I brought out silver platters of stuffed grape leaves and almond pastries.

"What's on your mind, Esther? Ask me for anything."

I wondered what to ask for. That the king make Haman chief of a remote island? Preferably one full of lions and surrounded by sharks?

No. Getting Haman out of the way wasn't enough. I had to stop his terrible plot, but this didn't feel like the right time to expose Haman as a villain.

"Will you both come for dinner again tomorrow?" I asked instead. "The cook has a new recipe for pomegranate-pumpkin parfait."

"We'd be honored!" Haman grinned at getting another royal invitation.

The next evening, when the king asked what I wanted, I spoke from my heart. **"Save my people. Save me."**

"Save you? From whom?"

"This wicked man. He plans to kill all the Jews in your kingdom. I am one of them."

The king turned to Haman. "You would harm my queen?"

Haman threw himself at my feet. "Please, Your Highness, I didn't know . . ."

The next day, Cousin Mordecai came to the palace gate waving a new order with the king's seal.

"Good news! The king has gotten rid of Haman, and his plot has been foiled!"

I'd outwitted the bully! When I was a girl daydreaming in my garden, I never imagined I would do something like this.

"This calls for a celebration!" I announced.

We're still celebrating. Every year, my story is told at Purim parties. It's not a fairy tale, though it starts like one:

Once upon a time, an orphan girl became queen . . .

And it has the best ending:

We all lived happily ever after.

A Note for Families

Every year on the holiday of Purim, we read the story of Queen Esther from a scroll called a megillah. We dress up in costumes and shake noisemakers to drown out the name of the villain Haman. We celebrate how Esther and Mordecai outsmarted Haman and saved the Jewish people.

But Esther did not know how her own story would go.

She did not expect to be crowned queen of a vast empire. She never imagined she would have to stand up and speak her mind to the powerful King Achashverosh. She was afraid, but she did what she knew was right. For that reason, Queen Esther is one of the great heroes of the Jewish tradition.

This book compares the story of Esther to the fairy tale of Cinderella. Esther and Cinderella were both orphans. Both hid their identity at the palace. Both were chosen to be queen in a sort of beauty contest. But Esther's problems were not solved by magic: She found the strength within herself. She also knew she had support from her cousin Mordecai and all the Jewish people.

None of us knows how our own stories will go. Things often happen that we don't expect or even want. Our problems are not going to be solved by magic. But we can find the strength to do what is right, especially with the support of our families and friends.

Were you ever afraid to do something you knew was right?
How did you overcome your fears? Did anyone help you?